THE DISGUISED LOVER

Borgo Press Books by FRANK J. MORLOCK

Castor and Pollux and Other Opera Libretti (Editor)
The Chevalier d'Éon and Other Short Farces (Editor)
Chuzzlewit
Congreve's Comedy of Manners
Crime and Punishment
Cyrano and Molière: Five Plays by or About Molière (Editor)
The Disguised Lover and Other Plays (Editor)
Doctor Scratch and Other Plays (Editor)
Falstaff (with Shakespeare, John Dennis, & William Kendrick)
Fathers and Sons
Herculaneum & Sardanapalus: Two Opera Libretti (Editor)
The Idiot
Isle of Slaves and Other Plays (Editor)
Jurgen
Justine
The Key to the Great Gate and Other Plays
The Londoners & The Green Carnation: Two Plays
Lord Jim
Mademoiselle Fifi and Other Plays (Editor)
The Madwoman of Beresina & Other Napoleonic Plays (Editor)
Mimi Pinson and Other Plays (Editor)
Notes from the Underground
Oblomov
Old Creole Days
Outrageous Women: Lady Macbeth and Other Plays (Editor)
Parades and Proverbs: Eight Plays (Editor)
Peter and Alexis
The Princess Casamassima
A Raw Youth
The Rose Princess and Other Plays
Salammbô & Dido: Two Operas (Editor)
The Stendhal Hamlet Scenarios and Other Shakespearean Shorts from the French (Editor)
Two Voltairean Plays: The Triumvirate; Comedy at Ferney
Whitewashing Julia and Other Plays
The Widow's Husband; and, Porthos in Search of an Outfit: Two Dumasian Comedies (Editor)
A Yiddish Hamlet and Other Plays
Zeneida & The Follies of Love & The Cat Who Changed into a Woman: Two Plays (Editor)

THE DISGUISED LOVER

AND OTHER PLAYS

FRANK J. MORLOCK, EDITOR

THE BORGO PRESS
MMXIII

THE DISGUISED LOVER

Copyright © 1982, 2003, 2013 by Frank J. Morlock

FIRST EDITION

Published by Wildside Press LLC

www.wildsidebooks.com

DEDICATION

To the memory of my friend, John Scanlon

CONTENTS

THE DISGUISED LOVER, by Charles Favart . . . 9
CAST OF CHARACTERS 10
THE PLAY 11
THE TRIPLE MARRIAGE, by Philippe
Destouches 79
CAST OF CHARACTERS 80
THE PLAY 82
RUSTIC AMOURS, by Charles Favart 161
CAST OF CHARACTERS 162
THE PLAY 163
ABOUT THE EDITOR 213

THE DISGUISED LOVER
OR, THE SUPPOSED GARDENER
by CHARLES FAVART

CAST OF CHARACTERS

JULIE, dressed as a lawyer

MADAME DE MARSILLANE, Provençal

LUCILE, daughter of Madame de Marsillane

CLITANDRE, lover of Lucile, dressed as a gardener, under the name Guillaume

MATHURIN, gardener

A NOTARY

The following characters are mute:

The COUNTESS

DAMIS, Julie's lover

And other persons in their company

Lackeys, gardeners, and other servants of the house who perform the diversions.

THE PLAY

The stage represents a decorated garden. To the right is a body of structures where a projecting balcony is observed. In the back is a pavilion whose ground floor offers a room where part of the action takes place.

JULIE (dressed as a lawyer)

What do you want, Mathurin?

MATHURIN

Madame!

JULIE

Call me "Sir."

MATHURIN

What? You, "Sir?"

JULIE

Yes, me, "Sir."

MATHURIN

Ah! The comical gentleman!

To deny one is a woman,

Having such a good heart!

JULIE

Call me "Sir."

MATHURIN

Ah, the comical gentleman!

JULIE

I intend to be obeyed.

Call me "Sir."

MATHURIN

To see this pretty face,

This enchanting look,

This envied pallor.

I defy

Every connoisseur

Not to shout out

Ah! The comical gentleman!

JULIE

Call me "Sir."

MATHURIN

Well! Yes, yes, Mr. Julie.

JULIE

Today that's no longer my name.

I am Counselor Vernon.

When I am in Paris, each moment exposes me

To see stupid lovers turn around me.

One has a free demeanor, and the other is composed.

They all have the jargon and manner of their employment,

And to say the same thing,

Each situation has its style of fidelity.

(Air)

When I flee to the country,

I mimic them in turn.

Gaiety always accompanies me,

I change dress each day.

Yesterday, officer young and slow,

Today, weighty lawyer,

And tomorrow, falsely modest,

I'll have the pinched air of a priest.

MATHURIN

That's to take a good role, but your mother-in-law

Wrote to warn you

That two Ladies must soon come here.

JULIE

Won't they go to her place first

To do the honors?

MATHURIN

Read: you are going to see.

JULIE

My brother is with her; they are expected tonight.

(reading)

"I announce this to you from the Countess de Marsillane. She ought to arrive tomorrow, but impatience to be married grips her; she has the Provençal vocation. You know that I've arranged it for your brother, who is only a cadet from Normandy. He will find a very rich, very pretty widow. She's bringing her daughter to scold her and not to marry her. I won't arrive until after supper because of the great heat. Perform many ceremonies for our Countess. Put into play all your gaiety, so that she will applaud herself for marrying someone whose sister-in-law is so agreeable." I am conceiving a plan. It's a prank. For my brother today, I intend to make love to her.

MATHURIN

That's playing the widow a nasty trick.

JULIE

My frivolity cannot, on this day,

Refuse itself this joke.

So, first of all, let her come;

Mathurin, beware of revealing me to her.

I shall play the gentleman.

MATHURIN

Perhaps,

Not as she would wish.

JULIE

I am burning to see her appear.

Don't betray me, be discreet.

I have a secret interest of my own.

MATHURIN (in a confidential manner)

You love pleasure.

They are giving her a party.

Hush—for the moment I have the thing prepared.

When my Mistress shall arrive—

JULIE

Fine! Fine!

MATHURIN

It's not necessary that one irritate her.

JULIE

No.

MATHURIN

Know yet another funny thing

A young and handsome Cavalier

Is disguising himself around here, and presenting himself at my place

In the capacity of a gardener-lad.

JULIE

Yes!

MATHURIN

He loves the daughter of this Countess greatly

They say she's truly fresh, lively, and sweet.

JULIE

Where could you know this from?

MATHURIN

The Gentleman's valet told me the thing.

JULIE

Why's he bringing him here?

MATHURIN

He told me the cause.

The master doesn't know how to take care of himself.

JULIE

The valet

Doesn't know how to shut up? Ah! What a role

I am learning to play! Put him in difficulties.

MATHURIN

Oh! Rely on me, I shan't fail.

(Clitandre enters dressed like a gardener.)

MATHURIN

Wait, wait, sir, here's this young wiseguy I was telling you about.

JULIE

I am sufficiently satisfied.

He has the shape, he doesn't have the manner of a workingman.

CLITANDRE

Sir—

JULIE

Yes, I like his looks well enough.

MATHURIN

But above all, it's necessary to examine him.

Find out if he is acquainted with his profession.

CLITANDRE (aside)

What to say?

MATHURIN

You must have some zeal,

And I will make an excellent model for you

If you become my assistant.

CLITANDRE

I love agriculture greatly.

I am coming here to observe

The riches of nature.

JULIE (ironically)

That you would like to cultivate.

How eloquently he speaks!

They might take you for someone of importance.

That's not the tone of a peasant.

CLITANDRE (aside)

Oh! I am betraying myself

(aloud)

From my most tender childhood

I received from my parents

An education; they were well off.

They lost their wealth and to avoid poverty

They made me take up a profession.

I made myself a gardener.

MATHURIN (aria)

A gardener is a great man

If he's properly made for his profession.

And he's a wise astronomer

If he's a good gardener,

Thunder and storm,

The results of bad winds,

Produce no ravages

If he knows the weather.

JULIE (always in an ironic and jesting tone; this constitutes the character of her part until the end of the play)

When he sees the amorous earth

Smiling in the Spring,

He seizes the moment.

He visits, he discovers

His new plants.

The yellow bud that's opening

Holds his caressing glance.

He contemplates, he admires,

You hear him say:

Tender flowers, appear,

Burgeon

The winds are peaceful

The days are sweet

Approach

Unite

Press tender hearts

To make them like you.

CLITANDRE

By boasting of this situation, you make it envied

And one is too happy to dedicate his life to it.

You make all its utility felt,

And that's indeed my plan.

MATHURIN

Are you really worthy of it?

Prove your ability.

Do you know in what weather you must cut the vine?

CLITANDRE

Why—that's in the month of January.

MATHURIN

Well answered, excellent worker!

Do you know peach trees and apricot trees?

Do you prune parasitic branches

Which don't bear any fruit?

CLITANDRE

That depends.

JULIE

He seems very informed.

CLITANDRE

But can you make these demands?

JULIE

Will you indeed tell me your name?

CLITANDRE

Guillaume.

JULIE

Ah! Guillaume is very good.

MATHURIN

How much do you want for wages?

CLITANDRE

Eh! Why, that depends on the work.

MATHURIN

If it's only that, I will give you some.

Work this five-part section; arm yourself with courage.

CLITANDRE (aside)

I am sure that I will expire

The first day of my apprenticeship.

JULIE

Mathurin, you must expose your taste.

Prune carefully your palisades

To make the promenades pleasing.

Let the rake pass everywhere.

Let them seek the concierge and each servant,

So the house will be neat, let them apply themselves

To make the floor shine

And to air out the rooms.

MATHURIN

You will be satisfied, sir, with my service

And I am going to assign to each his duty.

JULIE

And you, Guillaume, go match the carnations

With flowers of the rarest species.

We must make bouquets for the ladies.

In your job, that's politeness.

CLITANDRE

Today's not the first I understood flowers.

My natural ability

Gives me the talent to sort out the colors.

JULIE

You know that it's necessary to satisfy the beauties.

(he withdraws)

Here's the moment to take the detail

Of graces, of manners leading to please.

Let's play the important man; here's the only labor

Where one has no need of a secretary.

MADAME DE MARSILLANE

I can no longer keep myself from admiring the château.

The entrance is superb and the view is immense.

Assuredly in all Provence taste is refined; but it isn't new.

JULIE

Madame, I have the advantage

Of doing you the honors here.

The Countess is in the vicinity,

Doubtless with some great lords.

LUCILE (aside)

Clitandre as a gardener! Ah! I am confused!

O heaven! What lack of discretion!

CLITANDRE

Will I be able to control myself as I offer myself to her sight?

LUCILE (aside, noticing Clitandre, who appears at the back of the garden)

I am troubled!

MADAME DE MARSILLANE

Well! Now what are you gawking at?

You seem very upset to me.

LUCILE

I was admiring the way the garden's laid out.

JULIE (aria)

What a happy abode

Is the country!

Sweet countryside

Is smiling there at our prayers.

First off

You get acquainted with it.

Confidence is

Never mistaken.

Without effort, without upset,

Everything is leisurely.

The only abode

Is pleasure.

MADAME DE MARSILLANE

Yes, the country is ravishing.

But I don't limit my taste to it.

My humor is in all times sprightly and prominent

Depicting everything with its laughing color

And I take my part everywhere.

(aria)

I love the city, it's noisy.

I enjoy the whirlwind

And what makes me really content

Is the noise, the racket.

You run around all day

And at every step,

Fuss.

Look out, look out behind you.

A beautiful affectation

Puts your head out the door.

Shouting to the coachman, "Don't go forward."

At night they assemble for the spectacle

Followed by supping together.

Everyone's so falsely polite

And hates each other so gaily.

It's rapture,

It's a charming pleasure

Without the heart unbosoming itself.

Your head is scatter-brained,

You spend a white night

Without knowing what you said.

Dawn brings you back,

And you are quite surprised

To find that you hardly know

The name of your friends.

I love the city, etc.

(speaking)

Still, I find the house charming.

(noticing Clitandre)

Is that the gardener?

JULIE

You'll be satisfied with him.

He's a lad full of education

And who is very enlightened about his work.

And what's more, he has the air and manners

Of a man of condition.

MADAME DE MARSILLANE

Being here, apparently, from looking at him,

He's the best gardener in France.

JULIE

Guillaume, come forward, you aren't being gallant.

Come and show the garden to these ladies.

MADAME DE MARSILLANE

He seems indolent.

Are you astonished when you see ladies?

CLITANDRE

Madame, not at all.

MADAME DE MARSILLANE

He is embarrassed.

JULIE (aside)

I'm going to thrust him into it even more.

MADAME DE MARSILLANE

Lucile is just now turning her face away.

To laugh apparently?

LUCILE (uneasy)

Yes, mother.

JULIE

In any case

Laughter comes easily at her age.

MADAME DE MARSILLANE

The youth of today has no ready laugh.

In the old days, in Marseilles, when I was married,

There you could name gaiety.

I laughed, I laughed, oh, I split my sides.

JULIE (to Clitandre)

There, you are stiff as a pike.

Now what makes you so timid, Guillaume?

CLITANDRE (to Madame de Marsillane)

Madame, if I dared to offer you a bouquet?

MADAME DE MARSILLANE

With very great pleasure. What an aroma! It smells sweet.

Give it to my daughter.

CLITANDRE (low)

Ah! Lucile!

LUCILE (low)

You dare?

CLITANDRE (low)

I adore you.

JULIE

Only on one's knees

Should one offer flowers to burgeoning beauty.

It's the living image of the divinity.

Can one, by adoring her, attract her wrath?

Prostrate yourself, Guillaume.

CLITANDRE

Eh! Why—

LUCILE

The gentleman is joking.

JULIE

No, no, it's an established custom amongst us.

On your knees—

CLITANDRE

Here I am, since the gentleman orders it.

MADAME DE MARSILLANE

Truly, this boy astonishes me.

He has speaking eyes, his manner is so tender, so sweet.

That's enough, my boy, stand up, I am good.

CLITANDRE (to Lucile)

(Air)

I didn't dare

Say what I am thinking,

But I admire in silence.

And the distance

In our situations

Produces my shyness.

If some gardener-girl

Was offering me so many attractions,

Without fear of her anger,

I would tenderly tell her.

My love is intense,

My passion is constant.

I'm a gardener, I love

This portrait of Spring.

JULIE (to Madame de Marsillane)

What do you say about that?

MADAME DE MARSILLANE

Why—it sparkles with wit.

Ah! Nothing is so jocular!

Answer, my daughter.

LUCILE (aria)

When homage is sincere

It's always interesting;

And to succeed in pleasing

It needs no assistance.

Ah! If I were a gardener-lass,

Knowing your secret

I would cease to be proud.

My heart would forgive you.

MADAME DE MARSILLANE

Why, you are telling too much, child.

(to Clitandre)

That's enough.

JULIE (aside)

How embarrassed the two of them are!

MADAME DE MARSILLANE

These flower baskets seem carefully arranged.

Do you have bear's ears?

CLITANDRE (embarrassed)

Madame—

MADAME DE MARSILLANE

Seeing them, you'd think you were looking at velour.

No question, there are Hyacinth mixed in.

I intend to visit them.

CLITANDRE

You won't be able to see them.

Night is already lowering its veil.

(The stage begins to darken noticeably.)

MADAME DE MARSILLANE

As for me, I love gardens shining in starlight.

And nothing compares with evening silence

At that time all secrets are confided.

It's the moment of tender hearts,

The refreshing air, the quickening flowers;

And all my life I've been like flowers.

JULIE

Let's wait till tomorrow to pay the visit.

MADAME DE MARSILLANE

Well, in that case, willingly.

CLITANDRE

Finally, I'm out of it.

(he leaves)

LUCILE (aside)

Ah! My calm is coming back.

MADAME DE MARSILLANE

You are a professional,

Sir, it seems to me.

JULIE

I flatter myself on it, Madame.

MADAME DE MARSILLANE

Ah! How that pleases me!

There's not an instant you aren't robbed

When you're in a situation so brilliant.

JULIE

Eh! Why—?

MADAME DE MARSILLANE

The Countess is your relative?

JULIE

No, Madame, I allow myself

To do the honors in this house

When she is absent, under the title of friendship.

MADAME DE MARSILLANE

The thing is different.

The last title is much nicer,

Isn't it?

JULIE

It's a preference

That I deserve as much as I can.

MADAME DE MARSILLANE

I understand you; I'm sophisticated.

JULIE

Don't believe in appearances.

I swear to you I am

A man of no consequence.

MADAME DE MARSILLANE

Lucile, go to your apartment,

And take care of your fragile health.

LUCILE

Yes, mother, I'm going to sleep right away.

JULIE

Mathurin, Mathurin, promptly escort—

(Mathurin leads Lucile into the building with the balcony.)

MADAME DE MARSILLANE

I no longer recognize the youth of these days.

I've ruined myself with expenses caring for her.

Brought up in the best Convent in Paris,

Her education is far from being finished,

And she doesn't even pronounce French correctly.

JULIE

Madame, would I be lucky enough

To be of some use to you in Paris?

MADAME DE MARSILLANE

Ah! Sir, you delight me, I request that you

Follow the lawsuit carefully.

I'm an idiot in business matters

To a degree you cannot believe.

And I always give in to whoever argues with me

To avoid the boredom of defending myself.

JULIE

That's really having kindness.

MADAME DE MARSILLANE

(air)

All the girls in Provence

Under a pure and beautiful sky

See gaiety dancing

Around their cradle.

The first word they learn

Is the word "pleasure."

Their principal school

Is the art of grasping it.

When the weather dulls

The Springtime of desire,

From the fires of our dawn,

A spark still

Shines on our leisure.

From the fires of our dawn,

A spark still

Makes us say pleasure!

JULIE

I judge from this painting

That you don't know how to talk to Judges.

MADAME DE MARSILLANE

Ah! Fie! They give me the horrors!

JULIE

Do you really know what you must do?

Marry again.

MADAME DE MARSILLANE

Yes, that's prudent advice.

JULIE

A husband is but a Supervisor,

Trouble is his sole business.

Men are made to litigate

And women, on the contrary,

Are made to accommodate.

MADAME DE MARSILLANE

My spouse is found, since you must be told.

JULIE

To whom are you telling it? I am in the secret?

MADAME DE MARSILLANE

Honestly?

JULIE

The Countess has attracted you to these parts with him.

MADAME DE MARSILLANE

I see you are up-to-date.

JULIE

If your spouse had my physiognomy,

Would you have any antipathy?

MADAME DE MARSILLANE

I would love him like crazy

And from the first meeting

My heart would deliver itself to the sweetest inclination.

JULIE

Come on, then, kiss me, my dear intended.

MADAME DE MARSILLANE

What! It's you?

JULIE

Yes, tomorrow you will bear my name.

MADAME DE MARSILLANE

Now, that's the sole object of my ambition.

My daughter will be dumbfounded by the blow.

JULIE

Does she have some lover?

MADAME DE MARSILLANE

Yes, truly; soldiers,

She has many sighing,

Among which there's a certain Clitandre

Who I never see, he clings to his rank.

JULIE

That's a very good role, you can understand it

MADAME DE MARSILLANE

Yes, but among the aspirants,

The chevalier, Damon—

JULIE (excitedly and with emotion)

Damon cannot pretend to her.

MADAME DE MARSILLANE

Why?

JULIE

His heart is engaged.

MADAME DE MARSILLANE

Yes, his relatives told me that he loves one Julie.

A little flirt, pretty enough,

Who treats everything nonchalantly,

Seducing with her craziness.

JULIE

Don't speak ill of her, mercy.

MADAME DE MARSILLANE

Why?

JULIE

I have,

I have my reasons. They're very mistaken.

Her heart, firm and certain, belies appearances.

Julie and Damon's marriage has been arranged,

And it's I who take up their defense.

MADAME DE MARSILLANE

Since he is your protégé,

Clitandre shall have preference for Lucile.

Yes, but I really want to marry you first.

Without that, my daughter will taste of the convent;

Because, look you, I am making a big thing of marriage.

JULIE

Well, I think like you.

MADAME DE MARSILLANE

Yes! But the age difference:

Won't that be an obstacle between us?

JULIE

I will love you a thousand times more.

Reason and love will make me your spouse.

DUO

The flame of youth

Is only lit with pleasure.

MADAME DE MARSILLANE

At my age, tenderness

Is the talent to rejoice in.

JULIE

At your age, tenderness

Is the talent to rejoice in.

TOGETHER

The flame of youth

Is only lit with pleasure.

JULIE

I intend for you to give your daughter to Clitandre.

MADAME DE MARSILLANE

Since you esteem him, he will become my son-in-law.

JULIE

Happily for me, the Countess

Has made a notary come to draw up a lease.

She's going to return soon for this affair

And we will profit— But here he is, I think—

(Enter Notary.)

NOTARY

I learned some strange news as I arrived.

The Countess sent me here directly.

They say she's not at home.

I will return momentarily; my horses are not ready.

MADAME DE MARSILLANE

No, we need you,

You mustn't be in such a rush

And you have more than one contract to draw up here.

NOTARY

I mustn't defer it.

TRIO

MME DE MARSILLANE

Stay, sir.

THE NOTARY

Don't stop me.

You don't know

All my troubles.

JULIE

You must finish our business.

NOTARY

They are waiting for me at an Inventory.

MADAME DE MARSILLANE

A Marriage is worth more.

NOTARY

I have some wills to do.

JULIE

A marriage is more fun.

NOTARY

The bond of an heir.

MME DE MARSILLANE

Stay, sir.

NOTARY

A necessary reimbursement.

In the like case, in a similar case,

It's never put off.

JULIE

You must wind up our business.

No, no—you cannot go.

NOTARY

Don't stop me.

You don't know

All my troubles.

JULIE

Stay, Mr. Notary.

You must wind up our business.

NOTARY

They are pressing me

For ten contracts

Of life annuities.

A voluntary decree

About a house built like new,

Five beams of three, six, nine.

MME DE MARSILLANE, JULIE

Take a rest from your weariness.

Take care of our business.

NOTARY

Look, as for me, I'm sick over it.

Don't stop me, etc.

MADAME DE MARSILLANE, JULIE

Take care of your health.

NOTARY

I had the roughest ride,

Almost overturned a hundred times.

I am all shivering, and I fear the evening air.

I would like to warm myself promptly and sit down.

MADAME DE MARSILLANE

You certainly are a rare character.

JULIE

Don't forget Clitandre, at least.

MADAME DE MARSILLANE

I've given my word; is more needed?

NOTARY

Let's hurry.

MADAME DE MARSILLANE

Willingly, sir, that's my custom.

(to Julie as she leaves)

To hasten our pleasures, I am going to employ my

efforts.

(she leaves with the notary.)

JULIE (alone)

I couldn't serve Clitandre and myself better.

What a pleasure! I'm having fun making myself useful.

I'd like to laugh at their expense a little.

To make love uneasy is to stir up its flame.

(aria)

Love turns the fears of young lovers

To its advantage.

Makes 'em feel more tender and less fickle

Makes 'em feel the cost of moments;

Just a crossing cloud

Reveals sweet shining moments

And the alarms of youth

Are the storms of Spring.

(at the end of this aria night has darkened)

But already it's profound night.

The Countess with all her company

Can't delay coming.

Let's be sure everything is ready. But—hush, I hear them opening—

This announces some mystery.

Let's remain a bit to discover it.

(Lucile appears on her balcony.)

LUCILE

My mother is talking with a Notary in great secrecy.

Heavens! Did she bring me here to marry me?

My heart dreads to be enlightened.

(aria)

Why must they oppose

The sweet inclination of our passions?

The constraint they impose

Makes love more dangerous.

They want you to be faithful

To the one who torments our life!

They want us to be cruel

To the creature that forever pleases!

Why must they oppose

The sweet inclination of our passions?

The constraint that they impose

Makes love more dangerous.

(During this aria, Clitandre approaches the balcony stealthily, and Julie attentively listens.)

CLITANDRE

It's she that I hear, my heart is enchanted.

Let's profit by the darkness.

DUO (pianissimo)

CLITANDRE

Lucile!

LUCILE

Clitandre,

Walk on tiptoe.

They might hear you.

CLITANDRE

Lucile.

LUCILE

Talk low.

CLITANDRE

It's the tenderest love—

LUCILE

Speak very low, very low.

CLITANDRE

Do you love me?

LUCILE

I love you.

CLITANDRE

Alas, but you are fleeing me.

(hearing her shut the window)

CLITANDRE

What extreme weakness!

LUCILE

What extreme recklessness!

No, you don't love me. No, you don't love me.

CLITANDRE

I am not the dupe of this fright.

And you fear only that little gentleman

With long hair and a mocking air

Is not going to marry you; that's what's bothering you.

JULIE (aside)

Here I am in play.

LUCILE

No, no, be certain

That I feel nothing but indifference for him.

I would have married him with great aversion.

JULIE (aside)

See what instinct is.

CLITANDRE

So, you won't ever join together?

JULIE (taking the Provençal accent and counterfeiting the voice of Madame de Marsillane)

My daughter talking with someone in the garden;

That shocks me.

LUCILE

Ah! I tremble!

It's my mother.

JULIE

A child gives lots of trouble,

A daughter especially; she tortures herself, she cries.

Lucile, are you there? Go back in, I beg you.

It is late; at all ages, you must avoid the dampness.

No one answers. I'm afraid they will escape me.

(she seizes Clitandre)

It seems to me that a trick— Finally, I've caught you.

Why, it's not my daughter. Oh, stay put!

You must tell me who you are

On your secret strolls.

My penetrating glance is going to be enlightened.

CLITANDRE (taking Julie for Madame de Marsillane)

She's going to strangle me.

JULIE

Speak.

CLITANDRE

It's me, Madame.

JULIE

What! It's my dear Guillaume?

CLITANDRE

Yes.

JULIE

My best friend?

But Guillaume, ought, at present, to be asleep.

CLITANDRE

(aria)

I get up

Every night.

I'm afraid if I don't

They'll steal the fruits.

I interest myself

In my mistress.

It's my duty,

And I am coming to see

If some furtive hand

Isn't pillaging at night

The garden that I cultivate

And which is all my hope.

JULIE

Doubtless you receive very great advantages

From the employment to which you are committed?

I believe that as yet you have no wages;

You are content with the profits?

CLITANDRE (aside)

Will my secrets be betrayed?

I can no longer doubt it; the intrigue is discovered.

JULIE

His confusion rejoices me.

CLITANDRE

I have no other way to prevent my ruin

Except to steal off without any commotion.

JULIE

Oh! Stay, Mr. Clitandre.

CLITANDRE

Me, Clitandre!

JULIE

Yes, yes, the fact is not hidden,

And it's your valet who just spread it.

I think that this author is reliable.

CLITANDRE

Well! Madame, well! I admit it.

JULIE

Now there's frankness at last; I praise you for it.

I know indeed what I will do!

CLITANDRE

What do you mean!

JULIE

You are going to marry me!

LUCILE (on the balcony)

O Heaven, marry her! Ah! My mother,

I beg you not to do it!

JULIE (still counterfeiting the voice of Madame de Marsillane)

What! Miss, where are you hiding?

LUCILE

If you ever loved me,

Let Clitandre be my spouse.

I am coming down and I'm going to fall at your knees.

(Enter the Notary without being seen.)

NOTARY

It's choking because of the smoke.

I've ruined my eyes with it and I am suffocating.

MADAME DE MARSILLANE (without being seen)

This man always acts like he's offended.

Your contracts can easily be entered into.

NOTARY

Truly, they must want to hurry my departure.

MADAME DE MARSILLANE

Bring light to this room.

(She appears with the Notary and two lackeys, who light the room where the Notary has finished drawing up the Contracts. Meanwhile, Julie withdraws without being seen.)

CLITANDRE

To destroy her plan, let's not delay.

Madame, at your knees I beg a bounty.

(to Madame de Marsillane, thinking that it's she who just spoke to him)

MADAME DE MARSILLANE

What's this boy want? He looks disturbed.

CLITANDRE

Madame, truly, whatever effort I may make

I cannot decide on what you want.

MADAME DE MARSILLANE

He's lost his mind, judging by appearances.

CLITANDRE

On what are you basing that?

MADAME DE MARSILLANE

On what? What do you mean! On what?

CLITANDRE

I acted with frankness more than with prudence,

When I said, in good faith,

That I cannot respond to your love for me.

MADAME DE MARSILLANE

Mercy! Ah! What impertinence!

He needs to be locked up.

CLITANDRE

That marriage offends you?

You just now proposed it to me.

(Lucile enters.)

MADAME DE MARSILLANE

Against this lad, your mother is out of patience,

My daughter.

LUCILE

Your daughter, delivered to despair,

Dares to beg you not to marry him.

MADAME DE MARSILLANE

Marry him! This madness is universal!

JULIE (reappearing)

I wasn't expecting my rival who's here.

LUCILE

Mother, I would be so cruelly hurt by it,

Because he actually promised to be my husband.

MADAME DE MARSILLANE

Your husband! Guillaume?

LUCILE

Yes.

MADAME DE MARSILLANE

I feel my rage increasing by the minute.

As of tomorrow I will shut you up in a convent

To prevent such a disgrace.

(to Julie)

You, sir, you ought to take her glory to heart

Since soon you will be her stepfather.

LUCILE

Mother, you are going to marry this gentleman?

MADAME DE MARSILLANE

If you think it good.

JULIE

Madame, your mother

Has chosen much worse than you.

CLITANDRE

But, still, just now, I heard her—

Madame—

JULIE (imitating the Countess)

Do you want to know the truth?

It was I who took the liberty

Of laughing at your expense, my dear Mr. Clitandre.

MADAME DE MARSILLANE

Clitandre!

CLITANDRE

Yes, it's I; I cannot defend myself over it.

MADAME DE MARSILLANE (to Julie)

So you were counterfeiting my voice?

JULIE

From feeling.

To prove I am always thinking of the one I love.

MADAME DE MARSILLANE

You never say anything but what is charming.

Clitandre, I forgive this disguise,

I approve your intense love.

From this very day I give consent

To your marriage.

And tonight all four of us will go to get married.

Mr. Notary, come forward.

(The Notary, accompanied by two servants bearing lights, comes to have the contracts signed.)

JULIE

In a moment she might turn it down.

NOTARY

The two contracts are prepared.

MADAME DE MARSILLANE

Come on, my child, come on, sign you first.

LUCILE

Very willingly.

CLITANDRE

I am at the fulfillment of my wishes.

MADAME DE MARSILLANE (to Julie)

Now let's proceed to ours.

With what a good will I am contracting these bonds!

(signs)

I've signed. It's up to you.

(Julie signs)

What, you sign as Julie?

JULIE

Why, I have to, it's my name.

MADAME

That's not the name of a man.

JULIE

Truly, no.

I am, I certify it to you,

The stepdaughter of the house.

MADAME DE MARSILLANE

What a mistake! O Heaven!

JULIE

Console yourself. My brother

Should be arriving soon expressly for this affair.

MADAME DE MARSILLANE

Are you deceiving me again?

JULIE

I am his surety.

MADAME DE MARSILLANE

I refuse it. After a long widowhood

I wouldn't know how to enjoy a marriage

Whose proxy you bring.

MATHURIN (entering)

(aria)

Great rejoicing

In the village,

The Countess

Is returning to her château.

ALL

Ah! Good news!

MATHURIN

She's bringing with her

A really fine-looking lad.

MADAME DE MARSILLANE

Ah! Good news!

MATHURIN

He has a handsome figure.

He has nice manners.

JULIE

The thing is plain,

He's my brother.

MADAME DE MARSILLANE

It's your brother?

JULIE

Yes, it's my brother.

MADAME DE MARSILLANE

Goodie, goodie, goodie, goodie.

My heart's just jumping.

I am—I am ravished

Tomorrow I'm getting married

And all for the good.

ALL

Great rejoicing

For the village.

The Countess

Is returning to her château.

Ah! Good news!

Let's go meet her,

Singing and jumping for joy.

(The stage is suddenly lit up brightly. The Countess appears with Julie's brother and several lords and ladies. Julie presents Madame de Marsillane, Lucile, and Clitandre to the Countess. After having expressed their satisfaction, they seat themselves on the benches to enjoy the celebration that has been prepared. The entire last scene is in pantomime. The people of the château, gaily dressed, come in dancing to offer bouquets to the company.)

JULIE

For lovers and beauties,

Always sharp and tricky

Under a thousand new shapes,

You see love disguised.

Changing the sword for a pruning knife

The gentleman turns into a gardener,

To cultivate in secret

Some spring roses.

CHORUS

For lovers and beauties, etc.

CLITANDRE

To hide from his mother

Who he wounded with his darts,

Cupid, leaving Venus,

From Lucile took his features.

For this time I swear to you

That it was a bad plan

Under this pretty face.

(pointing to Lucile)

Love cannot be disguised.

LUCILE

I hid from myself

The gentle inclination of my heart.

But when you're in love, everything betrays you.

Cupid always conquers.

When you are tender and sincere

It's hard to pretend.

No, Clitandre, for you

My heart has no disguise.

JULIE (to the public)

They banished honesty,

Nothing appears in its day.

Today all is disguised,

Town imitates Court,

But our sincere zeal,

Gentlemen, is not counterfeit.

When one seeks to please you

The heart is not disguised.

(Provençals form an entrance and the Diversion ends with a general ballet.)

NOTARY

They're expecting me for an Inventory

I have four Wills to prepare.

The bond of an heir

A necessary reimbursement.

CURTAIN

THE TRIPLE MARRIAGE
BY PHILIPPE DESTOUCHES

CAST OF CHARACTERS

Mr. Matthews, an old man

Elizabeth, his daughter

Walter, his son

Mr. Manly, Elizabeth's husband

Anna, Elizabeth's maid

The Countess

Polly, Walter's wife

Sophie, Matthew's wife

Trim, Walter's valet

Jeremy, Manly's valet

Belinda, a little girl about ten years of age

Mr. Nugent

A Troupe of Dancers

THE PLAY

A room in Matthews' house.

Matthews

No, I cannot be perfectly happy. I had a wife and she died. Out of decency, I mourned her. Secretly, I rejoiced to be delivered from a tyrant who controlled my slightest breath and wanted to rule my inclinations after twenty years of marriage. I thought her death would leave me free.— Now, I am a slave to my children, who force me to go against my own wishes, and to preserve decency, without which I dare not proceed. I have to be careful my affairs are not noised about all over town. I have a son who is bigger than I am: what a mortification for a father who doesn't wish to renounce the world! I have a sweet and pretty daughter—who doesn't want to be a nun. So, to preserve decency, I have to marry her off. What an aggravating necessity for a father who loves his own comfort more than his daughter! What role should I play?— For the time being, better keep them amused, so as to have time to arrange matters in the way I wish.

(Enter Anna.)

Anna

What's going on, sir? I've just seen I don't know how many men down there getting drunk. What guzzlers! They've already emptied more than thirty bottles, and they complain they are dying of thirst. Who are they?

Matthews

They're dancers and musicians.

Anna

They drink like marines.

Matthews

Well, aren't they doing their job?

Anna

Only when they drink at somebody else's expense. I ought to watch them. But, sir, if you please, why have you brought this bacchanalia into your home? Are you giving a ball tonight?

Matthews

Yes, child, I intend to give a kind of ball tonight, or rather a little concert mixed with dancing. That's what

I brought these musicians and dancers for.

Anna

Better take away the drink, then, for if they continue as they've begun, you will have to carry them home.

Matthews

Never mind, don't worry about it—the more they drink, the better they sound.

Anna

Well done! And how were you able to bring yourself to have such a party—you, a sworn enemy to such diversions?

Matthews

I have reasons for it which everyone will learn before long. Besides, as my daughter is a little bored; I thought a little diversion like this would cheer her up.

Anna

It's true that music and dancing are pleasant, but I don't think this is exactly what your daughter needs to get her health back.

Matthews

Oh, I see where you're coming from. You mean she needs a husband!

Anna

Without a doubt. A husband is a sort of prescription medicine for a languishing daughter.

Matthews

I know my daughter: she's very virtuous.

Anna

Does it mean you can't want a husband because you're virtuous? On the contrary, it's her virtue which makes an honest girl want a husband. Those who are not so scrupulous have an easier time of it. I am going to prove that to you.

Matthews

I don't need your proofs.

Anna

Suppose, for example, you had walked a long, hot road in the summer heat.

Matthews

Well?

Anna

And that you were expressly forbidden to drink until you arrived at a resting place where they were waiting for you with agreeable refreshments.

Matthews

What an idea!

Anna

If you weren't forbidden, wouldn't you stop at an inn on the way? You wouldn't be in such a hurry to get there if you hadn't scrupulously observed the rule against drinking.

Matthews

I'll agree to that.

Anna

That's the exact picture of a young, emancipated woman. Elizabeth, on the other hand, is a traveler who observes the rules with such a scrupulous exactitude that she's reduced to the last extremity. Sir, remember, one cannot always withstand thirst, so it's unwise to put a young girl in the need of refreshing herself along the way by extending the journey.

Matthews

You're wasting your breath, I don't believe that eagerness to get it has caused Elizabeth's sickness.

Anna

Now, the doctors have lost their Latin for it, or rather, it's a miracle that despite their remedies she's still alive in such a perilous state.— I am not going to stop! She sighs night and day; she cries often; she falls in a languor—in a prostration which makes one fear for her life. Damn, sir, I know what I'm talking about. These are symptoms of an illness caused by love.

Matthews

You think she has some inclination in her heart?

Anna

I have not a doubt of it.

Matthews

Come on, come on, that cannot be. I am sure she herself doesn't know what an inclination is.

Anna

Ignorant at twenty-five in an age when girls are so precocious! Really, you cannot be so blind.

Matthews

I forbid you to say a word of this to her. You'll make her have ideas she doesn't have.

Anna

Oh, I wager she has an imagination more vivid than mine.

Matthews

I am going to plan this evening's party.

(Exit Matthews.)

Anna

Useless for him to dissemble; my speech exposed him, but I dare not yet hope—

(Enter Elizabeth.)

Elizabeth

Has my father gone? What did you tell him?

Anna

We spoke about your illness. We both rejoiced over your improvement.

Elizabeth

That was all?

Anna

You want to know if he spoke about your getting married?

Elizabeth

Shouldn't I think of it?

Anna

True, you're still a girl—and when one remains a virgin so long, one runs the risk of remaining one forever. I've offered your father some pretty thoughts on the matter.

Elizabeth

Did he seem to you more favorably disposed to my wishes?

Anna

Not at all. He believes you're still a child, and that you

can no more think of marriage than your sister Belinda.

Elizabeth

My mother warned me that if she died first, I would run the risk of not being married for a long time.

Anna

We indeed see the fulfillment of her prophecy. Death—miss! We must make an effort.

Elizabeth

What do you think I should do?

Anna

Tell your father how you feel. Tell him outright that he is stupidly deceived in the opinion he has of you—and that you're too much of a woman to remain a virgin much longer.

Elizabeth

I would never have the courage to tell him such a thing.

Anna

Then you must have the courage NOT to marry, and to wait patiently for the old man to die.

Elizabeth

I've made up my mind about that.

Anna

You could do something to help yourself, but you will never have the courage to do it.

Elizabeth

What could I do?

Anna

Cast your spell over some honest man, agree together, and marry secretly.

Elizabeth

You give me advice like that?

Anna

My word, Miss, one has to help save your life. When a father pays no attention to your needs—it is permitted to take care of oneself, if one can do it honorably. Don't waste your time pretending, I am sure you love Manly.

Elizabeth

I would have a lot to tell you if I were sure of your

discretion.

Anna

I'm a woman, but I can keep a secret. And, if you doubt it, I don't want to know anything.

Elizabeth

After all the proofs you've given me of your affection, I am sure you wouldn't want me to be lost—and lost I will be, if you tell anyone what I am about to confide in you.

Anna

I swear to you that your interests are more dear to me than my own.

Elizabeth

First of all, I swear to you that I love Manly with all my heart.

Anna

I never doubted that for a minute.

Elizabeth

And, I have promised to love him all my life.

Anna

You shouldn't make such a promise; a girl should never pin herself down like that.

Elizabeth (puzzled)

Why?

Anna

Because, a hundred to one, she will be unable to keep her word.

Elizabeth

I will keep mine with Manly.

Anna (maliciously)

You don't intend to marry him, then?

Elizabeth

To the contrary, I've promised never to marry anyone else.

Anna

My word, Miss, love and marriage have been divorced for a long time and have sworn never to live together. I hold their oaths are more likely to be kept than yours.

Elizabeth

Stop joking; Manly and I have found a way to keep in touch.

Anna

I wish it. Is that all you have to tell me?

Elizabeth

I tremble to tell you the rest.

Anna

Oh! Oh! I'm afraid you've quenched your thirst en route.

Elizabeth

What do you meant by that?

Anna

You know what I mean by it.— Continue!

Elizabeth

As Manly is my equal in birth, and besides has a considerable fortune, we agreed that one of his friends should go to my father without naming Manly as the person in question, to find out if my father would be willing to give me in marriage to a person who is perfectly suited to me.

Anna

Good.

Elizabeth

I cannot tell you how coldly he was received. In a word, my father absolutely refused everybody who was named.

Anna

Death! There's a father who deserves a daughter who will marry herself.

Elizabeth

Would you do such a thing?

Anna

Me? Ten times!

Elizabeth

Well, my poor Anna, I have already taken your advice. We've already secretly married— My aunt witnessed it at her house, where I am able to meet Manly. Unfortunately, my happiness won't last long. My father is alarmed at the frequent visits I make to my aunt. He has ordered me not to go there and has forbidden Manly to come here. I am in despair, and my fret has throne me into a sickness I think I'll die of.

Anna

I am delighted to know all this— And I want to help you— But what do I see?

(Enter Manly and Jeremy dressed as dancers.)

Jeremy

Come, sir, courage, we must kiss the hands of those two young ladies.

Manly

Shut up, you rogue, and think of showing some respect.

Jeremy

My word, I'm a little drunk. Drinking and respectfulness do not keep the same company.

Manly

I fear this bibbler will ruin my plans. What a misfortune to have need of you.

Elizabeth

Anna, who are these people?

Anna

They are two of the dancers your father has brought. They are dressed to amuse, apparently.

Jeremy

Yes, my ladies, we come to give you a little moment of sport.

Anna

I know that mug!

Jeremy

Mug! Oh! Mug yourself!

Manly (to Jeremy)

Will you shut up?

Elizabeth

What do I hear? It's Manly's voice— It's Manly that I see. Ah, Heaven!

Manly

Don't be frightened, Elizabeth. Yes, it is Manly who presents himself to you, and who cuts through insurmountable obstacles to obtain the pleasure of seeing you.

Elizabeth

You couldn't surprise me more agreeably. My joy is so great that I can hardly speak. But my happiness is cruelly crossed by the fact that my father will discover you.

Manly

I beg you not to worry; this disguise hides me from his eyes so effectively that he has no idea I am here—besides, he's seen me too infrequently to spot me in this get-up.

Elizabeth

And how did you get in?

Manly

I sent the dancers and musicians to your home and paid them some money to introduce me as one of their comrades. I thought it was wise that Jeremy play a role, too. Jeremy doesn't dance badly, and I only do passably well—and we ought to appear indistinguishable in the little divertissement that is being prepared.

Anna

And how can Jeremy help you? He is so drunk that he doesn't know what's going on.

Jeremy

Don't worry, I'm never better than when I'm drunk. On my oath, I was born to be a musician.

Anna

It would seem so. You're well adapted to your part.

Elizabeth

This man will infallibly give you away.

Jeremy

Eh! What a thing to say! Don't I know that your father is a brute who refuses to see my master—and that my master has a passion that forces him to see you despite your father. Therefore, for that reason, it follows—that my master must see you without your father seeing him. And me, like a discreet confidant—it follows that I must see you both while seeing nothing. Go, children, profit by the opportunity. Two make a party. Have a nice time together while I amuse myself with this hussy.

Elizabeth

Your valet makes me terribly nervous.

Manly

Rogue! If you give me away, I will give you a hell of a beating when we are outside—I cannot live without seeing you, my dear Elizabeth.

Jeremy

Nor I without kissing you, my dear Anna.

Manly

I will enjoy the happiness heaven grants me now, knowing the perfect felicity will be followed by a long period of sighing. But don't make me worry for your life, that is the bounty that I beg on my knees.

Elizabeth

Yes, I promise you, I'll be all right. Manly, get up—if you are caught in that position all will be lost.

Manly

No—I won't get up until you swear to me.

Anna

Peace! I hear someone.

(Enter Belinda, about ten years old.)

Belinda

Ah, ah, my sister, I caught you at it. A man at your feet. It's very cute—really, ha, ha, ha.

Elizabeth

Oh, I am in despair. She will tell everything to my father.

Jeremy

Plague on the little critter.

Anna

What do you want here, Miss?

Belinda

You don't think of me. You each have one of your own, but you leave me without one.

Elizabeth

What are you getting at, little scatterbrain?

Belinda

Hey, yes, yes, little scatterbrain. This gentleman here didn't whisper sweet nothings in your ear—and this one didn't kiss Anna? Mere tricks!

Jeremy

What do you want, little girl? If I understand you, I will give you a spanking.

Belinda

A spanking. Ah, ah—listen.

Jeremy

Yes, a spanking. Come one, bring me a switch right away.

Belinda

Look at this drunk who wants to give me a whipping.

Jeremy

Drunk! This little minx is too smart to live.

Anna

Listen, little girl! Don't go telling stupid stories. It's your father himself who invited these gentlemen.

Belinda

I am well aware he invited them. But to dance, not make love.

Elizabeth

What? You have the impudence—

Belinda

Come on, come on. I already know about THINGS. To be languorous, to throw himself at your feet, to kiss your hands tenderly, to cast dying looks—they call that making love—and I know perfectly well.

Manly

This little creature is very dangerous!

Belinda

I also caught my father doing the same thing this morning.

Anna

Your father?

Belinda

Yes, indeed. He was decked out like a young man. I

didn't say anything to him about it, but I watched him carefully.— When I'm big, I will remind him of it if he should try to prevent me from taking a lover.

Anna

Here's the most naughty little pest I've ever known.

Belinda

You're really irritated, aren't you, at what I've found out—for I can make you furious and revenge myself on my sister who treats me like a child, and who wants to be married before me.

Elizabeth

Well, you can get married first. Don't say anything.

Belinda

Good! I will marry first. You have the patience to wait till then? Come, come, sister, marry this gentleman quickly—then they will soon give me a chance to choose one for myself.

Elizabeth

Didn't I tell you that this gentleman is a dancer, and that I don't find him attractive?

Belinda

Hey, yes! A dancer! What a dancer!

Anna

Certainly.

Belinda

It's no use for him to hide behind his mask.

Elizabeth

Go on, you're crazy.

Belinda

Hey, no. I didn't see him down there drinking with the musicians; I didn't listen to him when he wasn't aware of it. He told them he'd give them plenty of money if they would pretend he was one of them— that he would be so upset, so upset, if my father saw him. Oh, if he's so afraid of my father, then he must be your lover—for my father doesn't want you to have any lovers. He's very wrong, because I think this is very amusing.

Elizabeth

How miserable I am!

Belinda

Go, go, fear nothing, sister, put your affairs in repose. I will prevent papa from coming here when he gets back—but, on the condition that you will help me when I get big.

Elizabeth

I swear it.

Anna

Me, too.

(Exit Belinda.)

Anna

That little girl promises much. A ten-year-old to discover a secret intrigue.

Elizabeth

I swear to you that I'm terribly nervous, and I believe that although you just got here, it would be better for you to leave.

Anna

And I, for one, think it isn't necessary. Count on Belinda saying nothing. Wait till she gets married. What a talent for pacifying a jealous husband. The man will be lost—for husbands in this country are the nicest in the world, and it doesn't take much skill to trap them.

Elizabeth

Anna, really!—it would be better if you kept your mind on how to help us, instead of giving vent to such silly ideas!

Anna

As you like. I am going to tell that precocious little girl not to say a word to your father.

Elizabeth

I will be very much obliged to you.

Anna

On my word, here he is himself.

Elizabeth

Oh, we are discovered.

Jeremy

Watch yourselves carefully.

(Enter Mr. Matthews.)

Matthews

Good day, my dear, how are you feeling?

Elizabeth

Not very ill today, papa.

Anna

I wager it was Miss Belinda who sent you here.

Matthews

Oh no, she didn't want me to come. She told me Elizabeth had left with you to take a walk in the Park.

Anna

That is what we spoke of doing in front of her, but Miss Elizabeth changed her mind because she is a little indisposed—and because she really loves dancing. I brought these gentlemen here while waiting for your little show.

Matthews

You did very well.

Anna

They are dressed to play a very exciting part.

Matthews

They both look good.

Jeremy

Sir, in all modesty, we are very light on our feet. (falling drunkenly on Matthews)

Matthews

Not so light, it would seem.

Anna

They are so drunk, both of them, that they haven't the strength to dance two steps. I told you exactly what would happen.

Jeremy

Frankly, Mr. Matthews, you really have the finest wine to be had in London, and if I weren't as sober as I am, I would be of half a mind to take good care of it.

Matthews

It seems to me, you haven't been too thrifty with it.

Jeremy

The better to amuse you. Wine gives me a strength, a

suppleness. Would you like to dance a little entrée with me, Mr. Matthews?

Matthews

No, no, my boy, you will do better to go sleep and wait till everybody's come.

Jeremy

You are a man of good counsel. Agreed! To sleep.

Matthews

I believe this one is not so drunk as the other fellow, because he doesn't say a word.

Jeremy

He doesn't think the less. My master has a sad mind.

Matthews

What—his master?

Jeremy

Hey, yes, sure! I am only his assistant. Wait till you see him. He's the best fellow in the world, and if you wish he will demonstrate with your daughter.

Matthews

Do you feel like trying it with him?

Elizabeth

I wouldn't dare suggest it to you, papa, but if you wish it, it would give me the greatest pleasure in the world.

Matthews

I retained you to show my daughter. She already has had good instruction.

Jeremy

So much the better. My master always wishes to add to his scholars.

Manly (pretending to be drunk)

Don't worry. I will impart to her all my—hic—skills.

Matthews

As soon as you can, I beg you. I've just decided to marry her off—and I want her to dance at her wedding.

Anna

And, to whom are you planning to marry her, if you please?

Matthews

To one of my best friends—we were students together.

Anna

With one of your school mates! Really, you're joking.

Matthews

What! Didn't you just tell me a little while ago that she needs a husband?

Anna

Yes, sir. But believe me—but my word, will a man who was your school mate be capable of restoring her to health?

Matthews

Mr. Nugent offers to take her without a dowry. I like that idea. He's coming here immediately, and I had better get ready to see him.

(Exit Matthews.)

Jeremy

Madame Nugent, I am your very humble servant.

Manly

Double-crosser! Is now a time to joke?

Elizabeth

Ah, Manly, what will become of us? Anna, help us with your advice.

Anna

I'm as flabbergasted as you, and what has just been said makes me even more so.

Elizabeth

Ah, if only my brother Walter were here! He loves me and father really cares about him. We could confide our secret to him and he would be able to help us. But he's been in the country for the last eight days and we don't know when he'll be back.

Jeremy

My God, what a mess you're in. But, I've found a way to get you out of it.

Manly

What good can you do us in the state you're in?

Jeremy

Wine gives me wit.— Silence, I am going to speak.

Manly

Let's see.

Jeremy

First of all, Miss Elizabeth must explain to her father, and do so with great discretion and charm: dear father, you don't know what you're saying or doing.

Anna

Beautiful beginning.

Jeremy

And secondly, you must speak to this old scholar who wants to marry Miss Elizabeth.

Manly

Well, what do I tell him?

Jeremy

You will beg him very kindly (for I wish to be kind to everybody) to leave here as fast as he can, but on the condition that he never return.

Manly

Nice thing to say.

Jeremy

So much the better if things fall out so that you don't have to do anything.

Manly

What's so much the better?

Jeremy

Yes, indeed. We won't soon be defeated. Because if he refuses to leave by the door, we must throw him out the window.

Manly

Oh, shut up, stupid—leave us alone so we can consider.

Trim's Voice

Tally-ho!

Anna

I hear someone. It sounds like Trim.

Elizabeth

If it's Trim, my brother isn't far away.

Anna

Return to your room, Miss Elizabeth. You, gentlemen, go join your pretended comrades. I wish to sound out Trim and learn from him whether or not Walter has some inclination. In that case, you have common interests, and I plan to unite them to upset your father's plans.

Elizabeth

Good idea. We must let her try. Her efforts may be useful to us.

Manly

You can count on being rewarded in proportion to the degree your services prove useful to us.

(Enter Trim, dressed for the hunt, with a hunting horn.)

Trim

Tally-ho! Tally-ho!

Anna

Eh! What's the reason for all this hunting noise? Have

you lost your mind, my boy?

Trim

No, my dear. I am just as clever as usual. Is Mr. Matthews home?

Anna

No.

Trim

Are you positive?

Anna

Absolutely certain! He would be very angry at your making such a racket.

Trim (walking about the stage)

Tally-ho! Tally-ho!

Anna

Ah! You'll be the death of me! Stop it, and don't bore me anymore. What devilish music is that?

Trim

Do you believe that Mr. Matthews heard me?

Anna

Without a doubt, and all the neighbors, too. (Trim blasts his horn) But, what do I hear? More noise of the hunt. Are we in the time of the fairies, and have I been suddenly transported into a forest?

Trim

Ah, my dear, I would love to find you in the depths of a dark wood.

Anna

Why? To cut my throat?

Trim

No, child, you wouldn't die of it. (another blast on the horn)

Anna

Why keep it up? What do you mean to do?

Trim

My master is hunting in his father's antechamber.

Anna

Would you mind telling me what this means?

Trim

It means that we make a noise.

Anna

Does your master wish to insult his father? Are you dreaming? Are you possessed?

Trim

Oh, be patient, and you will learn everything.

Anna

Hurry up then! What's going on?

Trim

We are trying to make Mr. Matthews think we have returned from a big hunting party in the country. We have just brought two mules home laden with game.

Anna

Two mules! What poachers! Did you depopulate the entire countryside?

Trim

Indeed, yes. We haven't left anything in the meat shops.

Anna

What the deuce are you talking about?

Trim

We were not at Cliffordshire Manor as we wish to fool old man Matthews into believing. We've only been to a village half a league from London, and we haven't even killed a sparrow.

Anna

What were you doing there for eight days?

Trim

The plague! Beautiful business, but it is a secret that I am not permitted to divulge to you.

Anna

Why not?

Trim

Because, my master has forbidden me to speak of it, and that's why I'm dying from the desire to tell you the whole thing. Oh, the heavy weight of a secret! Well— here it is—my master— Stop there, Trim, you are going to do something stupid.

Anna

You hide something from me—from your mistress?

Trim

I agree: that's not in the rules. But, at the same time, I have a thought: my mistress is a woman. Would she be a woman if she were not a person incapable of keeping her mouth shut and under the compulsion to reveal the greatest secret within twenty-four hours or die?

Anna

Don't worry. I—I am stronger than a man about discretion. Speak or I will break with you.

Trim

You take me on my tender side. All right, I've got to tell you. The greatest men engage in madness for these little bitches.— Nobody can hear us?

Anna

Not unless you speak loudly.

Trim

The devil! These are not childish games.

Anna

Well, then?

Trim

If someone discovers the mystery, my master will be disinherited—there it is, more or less.

Anna

The deuce!

Trim

And I, on the other hand, will inherit a beating. I don't like the idea of such a windfall.

Anna

You are only exciting my curiosity. Where have you been?

Trim

We were— Shh! Here comes the old man. I've got to pacify him adroitly on this subject. Leave us—I will join you as soon as I can.

(Exit Anna. Enter Matthews without seeing Trim.)

Matthews

To play me such a trick!

Trim (aside)

He seems to be in a rage.

Matthews

To try to put one over on me with such effrontery—a story like that.

Trim

Have we been found out?

Matthews

To have the audacity to say he came from Cliffordshire Manor.

Trim

The mine is blown.

Matthews

I wish to know if that devil Trim will also have the effrontery to pass this imposture off on me.

Trim

He knows everything.

Matthews (seeing Trim)

Please? Ah, you here. I'm very glad to find you, Mr. Scamp.

Trim

Good day, sir, how are you?

Matthews

That has nothing to do with your business.

Trim

Pardon, sir. The interest that I take in your precious health from the moment that I am separated from you, creates in my foreboding heart sentiments of the most lively tenderness, and delivers it into the turmoil of the excess of both tender and passionate emotions. Now, you are well, and I rejoice over it.

Matthews

Double-crosser! It's not a question of this gammon, you are telling me.

Trim

Anything you please. What is it a question of?

Matthews

Tell me where my son has been for the last week!

Trim

Didn't he tell you?

Matthews

He told me that he was at Cliffordshire Manor.

Trim

Well, that's the truth.

Matthews

Didn't I predict you would tell me that?

Trim

Yes, I said so, and I will continue to say so. When I tell the truth, I fear nobody.

Matthews

I have to admire the effrontery of this gallows-bird.

Trim (wishing to escape)

Oh—if you're getting irritated.

Matthews

Stay put, or I'll brain you.

Trim

Is there something I can do to serve you? You have only to speak.

Matthews

And you, you have only two choices to make.

Trim

Let us see.

Matthews

Take two pounds or be pounded on the head twenty times.

Trim

Simple choice. I'll take the two pounds.

Matthews (giving him money)

Here they are.

Trim

Thank you, sir. I wish you a good day.

Matthews (astounded)

You're going somewhere?

Trim

Yes, indeed. Didn't I choose?

Matthews

And have you told me what I want to know?

Trim

What, sir?

Matthews

Where did you spend the entire week? I know that it wasn't at Cliffordshire Manor. Clifford's aunt, the Countess, has come. She was staying with Clifford for two weeks, and she just told me that my son had not put in an appearance.

Trim

She wouldn't dare to say that to my face.

Matthews

That we'll see. She's still here.

Trim

Oh, if she's still here, I have nothing to say. I cannot tell a woman of her quality that she's crazy.

Matthews

You're trying to put me off the scent. But you won't succeed. I'm on my guard. Come on, tell the truth.

Trim

Oh, willingly! It's my character to tell the truth.

Matthews

You sanctimonious hypocrite!

Trim

So, to tell you exactly—

Matthews

The double-crosser is going to lie! But, reckon, that will serve nothing. I know where you were.

Trim

If you know, why do you ask me?

Matthews

I want to hear it from your own mouth.

Trim

Oh, fie, sir! Where is honor, where is probity? I give the word of a gentleman. Admit to me that you know nothing if I keep silent.

Matthews

If you keep silent, I will roast you.

Trim

They will be blows wasted. I have shoulders equal to any beating. I am of the race of sergeants and blows cannot frighten an illustrious member of my family.

Matthews

A singularly well-bred villain.

Trim

It is I who have an interest to make you admit that you are totally ignorant of where we have been.

Matthews

Why?

Trim

Because I am sensible of the honor. I want to be able to boast that you have caught me, and gained nothing from your money.

Matthews

Well, I admit that all I know is that you were not where you said.

Trim

You don't know anymore than that?

Matthews

No, that's the truth.

Trim

So much the better! May the plague choke me if I tell you anymore.

Matthews

You won't speak?

Trim

Here's your money. I have the right to keep my mouth shut.

Matthews

And, I have the right to brain you.

Trim

Strike. I will make you see that I have degenerated not one whit from the intrepidity of my forebears.

Matthews

His impudence leaves me helpless, and I know no more where I'm at than before. I order you to leave my house, and to never let me see you again.

(Exit Matthews.)

Trim

My word, I've had to withstand a rude assault—but, I brought it off like a gentleman. Now, let's look for my master. I have to instruct him.— Here he is in the nick of time.

(Enter Walter.)

Walter

What's the matter with you, Trim?

Trim

Nothing. Just thinking about a terrible beating I almost got because of you.

Walter

Because of me! And who is the rogue who wished to beat you?

Trim

Your honored father.

Walter

I don't understand a word. Are you joking?

Trim

No, indeed. The Countess of Cliffordshire has just informed Mr. Matthews that we were nowhere near her nephew's estate.

Walter

Ah, the old fool. She has sworn to make me unhappy. It isn't the only evil she has done me.

Trim

I know she's the devil.

Walter

You know she's been in love with me for the last two years, and she's mad for me to respond to her.

Trim

That's the truth! I've helped you deceive her a bit: you've had some narrow escapes.

Walter

Here, you see, she's coming to persecute me some more.

Trim

Leave her to me. I'll give her her walking papers.

(Enter the Countess.)

Countess

Well, sir, you've finally decided to stop hoping for me.

Walter

Me, Madame? I have no intention of giving you any

trouble.

Trim

He doesn't think you're the only one in the world.

Countess

I don't know about that! What's all this about your little hunting trip?

Walter

Madame, with your indulgence, I really don't have any story to tell you.

Countess

You don't owe me any explanation, little rogue! I can tell you better. You must tell me now where you've been for the last eight days. Are you pretending to me that you were with Clifford?— I'm waiting, faithless one, and I flatter myself that love will draw it from you.

Trim

Madame, he prayed for love to lead him, but unfortunately, they lost their way and became separated.

Countess

Eh! You should have followed love, ingrate! How could

you be in league together, when I wasn't there?

Trim

They didn't know their way, Madame. Or me either. Love is blind, I hear tell—and when one takes love for a guide, it's easy to get lost.

Countess

All this gallantry is useless. I want him to answer my questions himself.

Walter

It suits you, Madame, to reproach me—after all you have done to embroil me with my father. If my absence bothered you, you should have had an explanation with me—I would have explained everything. But, after the service you have just done me, I will tell you plainly, you will learn nothing.

Countess

I will learn nothing! You will explain to me or I will strangle you.

Trim

Let it go, Madame—he's a bullhead, and won't say a thing. I will respond to you; I will interpret his thoughts.

Countess

Well—speak, and I will recompense you in accordance with your sincerity.

Trim

You have a very tender feeling for him.

Countess

So much, you cannot imagine. I lose my wits, my poor Trim.

Trim

It's apparent. You want him to respond with a tenderness equal to your own.

Countess

Haven't I the right to expect it?

Trim

There are pros and cons to this business. He knows how you feel toward him. He's a very penetrating fellow. There it is, Madame, I wager a hundred pounds against you that he can never love you.

Countess

He can never love me, villain? I don't know what prevents me from scratching your eyes out.

Trim

Softly, if you please. It is not I who am insensible to your charms—on the contrary, I find them very—piquant—although they're not of the first edition.

Countess

He can never love me! (to Walter) Is he speaking the truth, perfidious wretch?

Walter

Madame, in truth—I am in confusion, if my heart were—Trim, explain all this to Madame La Comtesse.

Countess

He can never love me!

Trim

No, Madame, but it's your fault, not his.

Countess

It's my fault—after all that I've done?

Trim

That's true. We don't disagree. But the fact is, you have such nobility in your looks, such majesty, and I don't know what that's grave and imposing—that it can only inspire him with esteem and respect. Love doesn't rub off from such venerable personages.

Countess

If my features inspire him with respect, my glances ought to inspire him with love.

Trim

That's where we disagree.

Countess

You cannot disagree.

Walter

Hold, Madame, I've great obligations to you; I am too gallant a man not to speak to you sincerely. Let me then disabuse you, and say to you, with all respect, that I owe you that.

Countess

Don't finish, you double-crosser. I know where that little speech is going to end.

Trim

But, you are very wrong, Madame.

Countess

I am wrong, me! I am wrong! In what respect, if you please?

Trim

You're wrong to come into the world twenty years before he did. Why were you in such a hurry? If you loved him with so much tenderness, you ought to have planned ahead, and seen to it that he was born five or six years before you.

Countess

That depends on me?

Trim

No, Madame. But it doesn't depend on him to love you.

Countess

Then, why was it necessary to deceive me with false protestations?

Trim

They were not his.

Countess

And, whose then?

Trim

His father's, who let it all happen. You offered to help him in his needs. The occasion was pressing. He saw a way to profit by your generosity. For recompense you wanted signs of love. The poor boy put himself to incredible expense in sighs and protestations. You treated it as a trifle, and he had no other coin to pay you in.

Countess

You say not a word to this, sir?

Walter

My word, Madame, he who makes no protest consents.

Trim

Would you like me to tell you a way to revenge yourself on him?

Countess

You would give me a great satisfaction, because I am beside myself.

Trim

And I, I who speak to you, I am in a rage against him. Let's stand a little further off.

Walter

What the devil's he going to say to her?

Trim

What are you looking for in a husband, Madame?"

Countess

A nice young man.

Trim

Well, I am your man. I will marry you, if you wish.

Countess

Get away from me, you wretch!

Trim

I will avenge you better than anyone else.

Countess

Get out, I tell you—I have a more sure way to punish this infidel.

Trim

That's what I'm afraid of.

Walter

And, what have I to fear?

Countess

Everything. I am going to marry you, in spite of yourself.

Walter

Marry me! Ah, Madame, you wouldn't be as cruel as that.

Countess

Yes, perjurer! I have just asked you from your father. I offered to take you without a penny. My proposition was agreeable and he accepted it, and that is enough for me. Goodbye, sir. Think about it. But, get it in your head that I am to be your wife. I have sworn it—it will be—and I am the one who tells you so—and I am your very humble servant.

(Exit Countess.)

Trim

She's woman enough to do just as she said—at the very least.

Walter

What a mess the crazy old fool has put me in.

(Enter Elizabeth and Anna.)

Elizabeth

Oh, brother dear, I really need your help.

Walter

Oh, sis, I really need your help.

Elizabeth

My father has put me in despair.

Walter

My father wishes me to die of sorrow.

Elizabeth

Papa intends to marry me to Mr. Nugent.

Walter

He wants me to marry the old countess.

Elizabeth

I'll die if I do it.

Walter

I'll die if I don't resist him.

Anna

Here's a good beginning. Our fortunes are parallel—and don't they resemble each other in other respects?

Walter

Ah, Anna! My sister has less to complain of than I. She lacks the strength to resist—and she will end up living with a man she has the right to hate; but my fate is more cruel. For, I cannot follow father's orders or explain to him the reasons that prevent me from doing so.

Anna

We are in the same boat!

Walter

How can that be?

Anna

Explain yourself a little more and we will do the same.

Elizabeth

Brother—hide nothing from me, I beg you.

Walter

Ah, sister; I dare not speak. The slightest indiscretion and I am lost.

Anna

Same here. A single word is capable of ruining everything.

Elizabeth

Brother, do you believe I am capable of betraying you?

Walter

I can't conceal anything from you—Trim—tell her what has happened. I haven't the strength to do it myself.

Trim

Me, sir—reveal a secret! You take me for someone else.

Walter

All that I will admit—generally—is that I cannot marry from now on.

Elizabeth

Alas, brother, it is no longer permitted that you consent to the marriage proposed for me.

Walter

The hardness of my father has constrained me to certain measures which I am unable to take back.

Elizabeth

The same reason has put me under the necessity of consenting to engagements which can no longer be broken.

Walter

I am already married, sis.

Elizabeth

I am already married, brother.

Walter

Ah, heavens, who is your spouse?

Elizabeth

Manly.

Walter

Manly—I know him. He's one of my friends.

Elizabeth

And who is the wife you have taken?

Walter

Julia. Miss Prescott.

Elizabeth

I know her. She's a darling.

Anna

So, the confidence has taken place.

Elizabeth

What role do you play, brother?

Walter

That of exposing myself to everyone rather than break my marriage vows. And you, sis?

Elizabeth

To die, rather than break my word.

Anna

Here comes your father, with the Countess and Mr. Nugent.

Walter

I tremble.

Elizabeth

I can't any more.

(Enter Matthews, the Countess, and Mr. Nugent.)

Matthews

Here they are—both of them. I am going to make them agree to the projects we've formed.

Countess

Here's where you must employ all your parental authority.

Nugent

For myself, I make no pretence to the hand of Miss Elizabeth, unless she gives it to me from her heart.

Matthews

Oh, it's you, the huntsman. When will you return to Cliffordshire Manor?

Walter

Father, if you will only listen to me.

Matthews

I don't have to listen. To mend the wrong you've done me, you must prepare to obey me.

Walter

If what you order me to do is possible—if not, then I can't do it.

(Enter Belinda.)

Belinda

Papa, there are, I don't know how many maskers who have just come in because they heard the violins. They are very nice. Do you want to let them come here?

Matthews

They are very welcome. On a day like this, we must think only of spreading joy.

(Enter Julia, Manly, and other Maskers.)

Countess

The assembly is not numerous, but it is agreeable. Come here, Walter, here is a happy day for you.

Matthews

Assuredly, a happier one than he deserves.

Countess

You've been told my intentions.

Walter

Madame.

Countess

Now, I will marry you. All your rivals will die of jealousy—but you deserve victory. As for the rest, your esteemed father has given his word for our marriage.

Nugent

And, he promised me, too, Miss, that I will have the honor of marrying you.

Matthews

Say something.

Countess

He's so overwhelmed with joy that he lacks the strength to thank me.

Nugent

Missy doesn't seem to me so rejoiced by the news I've brought her.

Matthews

We'll speak of that later, Madame. Let's think of our entertainment.

Countess

No, if you please, I want to finish. I only dance when I feel like it.

Walter

If you're in such a hurry to finish, Madame, I will take the liberty of saying to you, with my father's permission—that I do not at all wish to get married.

Countess (grandly)

All that is useless.

Walter

I have great respect for you, Madame—but that is all your person inspires me with.

Matthews

It isn't a question of love or respect. The offer Madame made to me was so advantageous for you, and for me, that you cannot do better than marry her.

Walter

Does self-interest oblige you to render me miserable? Cast a father's eyes at me, and don't drive a son who throws himself at your feet to despair. For I am resolved to die a thousand times rather than let myself be mercilessly sacrificed.

Matthews

Get up, rogue, you will wait for me.

Walter

I won't get up unless you hear my reasons.

Matthews

I'm sure they're good ones. But I've given my word to Madame. As for that, I don't wish to force you to marry her—but I beg you to resolve this out of love for me. Can you refuse a request asked by your father?—When he has the right to make you obey him?

Walter

Heaven is my witness, I have tried to conquer my distaste and to respond in kind to such a soft and obliging proceeding; if it still depended on me to comply with your wishes in this—but you force me to tell you, before the whole world, that I am not free and my word is pledged forever.

Matthews

Forever! Without my consent?

Walter

Only consider the difficult step I have just taken. You never wanted me to marry. I have taken a wife without your consent. My uncle and all my relatives advised me to do it. And it was in their presence that I married Julia, Miss Prescott, a week ago.

Matthews

I'm delighted to know that, Mr. Rogue; I know what measures I must take.

Walter

All your measures will be useless. I pray heaven to destroy me, if I ever take another wife, except Julia, Miss Prescott. All the world knows Julia—Miss Prescott—to be wise and virtuous. She had noble birth and a fortune large enough so that we can live comfortably without having a charge on you. The whole world is ours.

Matthews

It infuriates me to agree he's right, and that I cannot disapprove this marriage without injustice.

Countess

Well! I can break it, even if you are crazy enough to approve it.

Walter

And, by what right, Madame, if you please?

Nugent

Believe me, Madame, it's better to swallow the pill quietly.

Countess

Wait and see. He will marry me or I will have him abducted.

(Exit Countess.)

Matthews

Let her talk. It's a woman speaking. Anna, go find Julia. When you cannot prevent things, you have to accept them with a good grace. I am going to tell her myself that I recognize her as my daughter.

Julia (unmasking)

Here I am, sir. Let me receive this precious title and tell you that I will do everything possible to be worthy of it.

Matthews

Ah, my daughter-in-law was in the masquerade.

Be welcome, Madame. It's not necessary that I say anything more to you as you've overheard everything. Julia I am touched by your kindness, and you will never regret it.

Walter

What a recompense I owe you father.

Matthews

Forget the sweet talk. Let's enjoy ourselves by celebrating another marriage, the one between my daughter and Mr. Nugent.

Anna

Now, it's your turn, Miss. You must jump the ditch.

Elizabeth

While you're disposed to pardon, father, and since you've shown so much indulgence to my poor brother and Julia, let me ask you for the same grace.

Matthews

What now?

Elizabeth

I don't love this gentleman. If my life means anything

to you, don't force me to marry him. I've thought about dying for a long time during my illness—which was brought on by your refusal to let me marry Manly. Be sure I am going to die at your feet if you don't approve my marriage to Manly as well.

Matthews

If I don't approve the marriage! You're secretly married, too?

Elizabeth

It's with great confusion that I admit it. Yes, father, Manly is my husband. I've been married to him for the last six months, and my aunt who has a fortune wished to unite us together.

Matthews

Your uncle, your aunt. By God, I'm indebted to my brother and sister for the care they take of my children! Well, here's an affair for which there's less remedy than the other. Mr. Nugent, I cannot break this marriage without dishonoring my daughter.

Nugent

There's nothing for me to do but leave this honorable company.

(Exit Nugent with a cold bow.)

Matthews

Come, come, I am well aware there's nothing I can do. Let someone tell Manly that I accept him as my son-in-law—but on condition that he gets nothing from me until I die.

Manly (unmasking)

I accept this condition with all my heart. I'm very happy you deign to give me Elizabeth, who is worth a hundred times more to me than all the wealth in the world.

Matthews

Oh, my dancing master, you demonstrate to my daughter without my permission?— As for that, children, I pardon your faults and your follies, provided you pardon mine.

Walter

What's that mean, father?

Matthews

I am secretly married, too. Me, your modest father.

Trim

Without our consent?

Matthews

I didn't wish to declare the business for fear it might upset you, but this development mutually excuses all.

Walter

Let's see our stepmother, and we will receive her with all the tenderness and respect we owe you.

Matthews

She is also in the masquerade, and it was for her that I planned the party. Deign to unmask, Madame, and take these young marrieds for your children.

Sonia (unmasking)

I'm very happy to enter into so lovable a family. I hope they are as happy as I am to be their mother.

Trim

Anna, shall we give our consent to this marriage?

Anna

One could criticize it. But, come, it's necessary to grant a general amnesty.

Belinda

Papa. I have one more blessing to ask you.

Matthews

What? My God, wench, are you secretly married, too?

Belinda

No, no, Papa. I don't want to be married except by your consent. So I bet you; it would be so nice.

Matthews

We shall see in a few years. Good Lord, it's a rage that runs through the entire family.

Trim

The company is getting impatient. Let the entertainment begin.

CURTAIN

RUSTIC AMOURS
BY CHARLES FAVART

Special thanks to Horvallis for helping me with some difficult passages in this and other plays.

CAST OF CHARACTERS

PHILINTE, a shepherd

HELEN, a shepherdess

LISETTE, a shepherdess

DAMON

RICHARD, laborer

SHEPHERDS, SHEPHERDESSES

PEASANTS, PEASANT GIRLS

THE PLAY

The stage represents an agreeable countryside; on one side is a hill covered with trees, and on the other a prairie cut by streams.

PHILINTE:

Our shepherds are going to the sound of bagpipes

To celebrate the village fest:

To calm and innocent pleasures

All hearts are soon going to be delivered.

I will be the only one in these retreats

That an ingrate is causing to sigh.

Already I can hear their plain song

Resound in the plain and the hills.

LISETTE:

Philinte, tell me your wrongs,

Your pain interests me.

PHILINTE:

Dear Lisette, two rivals

Alarm my tenderness.

Helen has a thousand looks for them

And seems to avoid my glances.

A fat farmer from this village and

A little dandy from Paris

Are smitten with my shepherdess.

LISETTE:

Go, don't take any umbrage.

PHILINTE:

They are more opulent than I.

LISETTE:

Do they know how to love like you?

One is a fat rustic lover

Whose love abruptly is stated

And the other a gallant puppy

Only touched by the taste of pleasures

And who seems, when he speaks, to complain

Of fatigue from opening his mouth.

PHILINTE:

When I played a new tune,

Soon my shepherdess came

At the sound of a rustic flute

To join her light voice.

Now I vainly make up tunes.

I've made tunes expressly for her,

And the faithless one

Is singing other songs.

Helen was so proud

To wear my first bouquet

That she used it to adorn her corset

For a whole week.

Today I gave her bluebottles and

She hid them under her kerchief;

And when she saw my rivals

She tore 'em off.

LISETTE:

What you are telling me, shepherd,

Seems very strange to me.

PHILINTE:

My heart would like to free itself

Since the ingrate is changing.

But whoever loves her need never fear

Of ever breaking his chain.

Eh! What object has more attractions

Than perfidious Helen.

I love an ungrateful beauty,

And it's for all my life.

I no longer have any willpower,

My freedom's ravished from me.

Helen is harsh,

But my heart prefers her harshness

To the sweetest favors

Of all the other shepherdesses.

When in the field, during the morning,

The distant troupe calls her,

Heaven becomes more serene,

Dawn rises with her,

Flowers are seen to bloom,

To die, on her breast.

At the dazzle of her complexion

The rose blushes.

The nightingale's going to sing,

Joyous at seeing her so beautiful.

The darting butterfly

Mistakes her for a new flower.

The amorous zephyrs

Are born from her breath

And my ardent sighs

Follow her in the plain.

Despite her timidity,

Which renders her even more beautiful

From a tender sensuality,

I've seen Aurora in her eyes.

And her mouth expresses,

With a charming smile,

The sweet pleasure of loving

What she fears and desires.

LISETTE:

Let's pipe down, I see your rival,

My little dandy, coming.

Let me talk to him.

Beware appearing.

I will know how to serve your passions.

PHILINTE:

I'm counting on your zeal.

What a ghastly torture

To love an infidel.

(Exit Philinte, enter Damon.)

LISETTE:

He's still getting dressed.

DAMON:

(pocket mirror in hand, he's adjusting his hair)

What a nuisance to fix!

Ah! There you are, beautiful Lisette.

What! Here without a shepherd?

By the way—

LISETTE:

What?

DAMON:

(continuing to arrange his hair)

Have you seen?

LISETTE:

Who?

DAMON:

The little one?

Her face is original.

She's not bad,

Not bad at all.

LISETTE:

You're looking for Helen here?

DAMON:

The hussy is worth the trouble,

And her innocent charms

Are offering me the laughing image

Of nature being born

In beautiful days of Spring.

LISETTE:

But Richard, that fat workman,

Can battle with you for your lover.

Are you sure that your passion—?

DAMON:

Am I sure? How charming she is!

Be the judge, look at me

And at the same time, consult your own feelings.

LISETTE:

All must grant you victory.

DAMON:

Little Helen has the glory

Of softening me up.

She has a thousand attractions for her share,

But she's always so wild.

It's deathly.

Tell her to humanize—

LISETTE:

But her modesty?

DAMON:

What stupidity!

Pain exceeds the pleasure.

With us the vainest beauty

Answers to our first sigh,

Pleasure exceeds the pain.

I intend to adorn her heart,

To lead away the shepherdess;

I know that at Paris her modesty

Is going to make her seem foreign.

But in about a month,

I'll certify it to you,

I'll know how to give her the manners

Of the best company.

LISETTE:

Ah! How charming her fate will be!

(repeat)

You are going to limit your desire

To loving yourself all your life.

DAMON:

Frequently, a moment is enough.

What's the use of forging chains

And limiting her in her desires?

All love has for fidelity is trouble,

For inconstancy, it has only pleasure.

Can you think that a passion

Can last for such a long while?

Who intends to subdue my soul

Had better profit by the opportunity.

Find Helen and inform her about it,

And tell her I'm waiting for her.

LISETTE:

Wait for her under the elm.

DAMON:

Here's the picture of happiness.

When champagne, full of passion,

Laughs and sparkles in my glass,

It's a moment that must be seized,

Or soon its flighty froth

Will disappear with the pleasure.

(Damon leaves.)

LISETTE:

Philinte is wrong to be worried

About the love of this little dandy.

As sure as I know myself

He loves himself too much to be loved.

RICHARD:

(singing but not seen as yet)

Love's makin' me, la, la, la,

Love's makin' me die.

LISETTE:

I see Richard coming

From the fields.

RICHARD:

Helen, dear Helen,

How you make me suffer!

Love's makin' me, la, la, la

Love's makin' me die.

(Richard appears.)

RICHARD:

Nothing can cure me.

Ah! There you are, Lisette.

Would yuh really like t' help me

With my brunette?

I'm havin' recourse to you.

LISETTE:

Very willingly, very willingly.

RICHARD:

My dear,

I'm sharing the wit

And the appetite.

LISETTE:

What must be done for you?

RICHARD:

Helen's looks,

Which the dog of love makes game with,

Have in my breast set all aflame.

But like a zephyr,

Which plays around a flower,

Her charming smile

Refreshes my heart.

By jimminy, it's a rage.

Day in, day out, they see me waste away.

I had no courage

Except to love

For my labor.

Dammit, instead of freeing me,

My greatest output

Is to sigh.

LISETTE:

Does she have a preference

For someone else?

RICHARD:

No, doggone.

I am not less puzzled.

I wanted some assurances,

And when I demanded them—

LISETTE:

Well?

RICHARD:

Her only response was curtsies.

Zounds! That's well and good,

But all that doesn't guarantee nuttin'.

First off, I had some notion

That your big cousin Philinte

Had obtained a return from her.

But I saw that, like a smart girl,

She avoided this vicinity

After she had my love.

I watch her everywhere carefully.

LISETTE:

And you are not doing so bad.

RICHARD:

I wouldn't be joking

If I had someone for a rival.

Since Helen is in her springtime,

She must make use of it in the usual way.

Make her understand the time's come

For her to set up a household.

Does she always intend

To be so miserly of her friendship?

And to let her little heart—what a pity!—

Lie fallow like this?

Man's the supporter of woman.

Zounds! She'd be nothing without him.

I'm giving a good lesson

To vines in need of support.

Females are like vines:

Without support they're good for nothing.

LISETTE:

Near the vineyards of our girls,

You see mischievous fellows prowling.

To be sure of them, you must pick

The grapes as soon as they ripen.

To harvest before it's ripe,

All the Gentlemen are on the lookout.

The sparrows come to pilfer;

The stalk is what remains;

Above all beware a pilferer.

RICHARD:

Who is it?

LISETTE:

He's a little gentleman,

Whose heart Helen has won.

I would never have believed he did it.

He made me privy to his triumph.

RICHARD:

What's that, that little libertine

Intends to do me outrage!

I will ring the tocsin

On him in the village.

Ah, doggone it.

By Jove.

Sonofagun.

I'll make a fine uproar.

He's only a little pipsqueak,

Only good for cackling,

And I'm going to send him packing.

(Exit Richard.)

PHILINTE:

(entering) Well, do you know if my ingrate

Was able to betray me?

LISETTE:

Each of your rivals flatters himself

He's obtaining her.

But here we don't know

The art of changing.

And to suspect a shepherdess

Is to outrage her.

I see Helen coming.

Question her heart.

But, in depicting your passion,

Hide your pain from her.

(Exit Lisette, enter Helen.)

HELEN:

(aside) What's so annoying

As controlling oneself?

Must I hide my flames for a long while?

My tender heart is ignorant of the art of dissimulation.

What's so annoying

As controlling oneself?

Must I hide my flames for a long while?

(Seeing Philinte, she wants to withdraw.)

PHILINTE:

Stay put, my shepherdess.

I was seeking you hereabouts.

Your presence is dear to me.

Ah! Don't deprive my eyes of it any more.

Absent from you, I am languishing,

When I see you I am reborn.

HELEN:

What do you want from me, Philinte? Alas!

Your love disturbs me.

Please don't follow my steps.

I want to be alone

Watching my flock,

Turning my spindle,

Singing my song.

PHILINTE:

You deigned to soften

At the recital of my pain,

And now you want to flee me!

Hey, what did I do to you, Helen?

Ah! Inhuman shepherdess,

Your harshness is causing me to die.

These tender flowers that decorate the green

Have perfumed the breath of zephyrs,

With this beautiful day the light is more pure.

In our hamlets all is given over to pleasure

When Spring reanimates nature.

Alas, I alone, I'm expiring of languor.

But take pity on the pains I'm enduring

And Spring is going to be born in my heart.

HELEN:

No, no, Philinte,

Let's no longer love, let's break our dangerous

Fetters.

Fear always

Disturbs amorous hearts.

(aside) His sad complaint

Makes me suffer too much.

(to Philinte) I cannot cure

The languor with which your soul is seized.

No, no, Philinte,

Let's no longer love, let's break our dangerous

Fetters.

Fear always

Disturbs amorous hearts.

PHILINTE:

Hear the warbler

Animating itself with its songs.

It's telling you:

Brunette,

Loving is a pleasure.

HELENE:

The sighing pigeon

Seems to tell me,

With its shivering,

Love is a torture.

PHILINTE:

See the shadow with this trembling?

Two butterflies

Flying together;

They are forming two whirlwinds.

Love by itself brings them together.

Everything depicts love.

To our hearts hereabouts

Everything is love.

HELENE:

I saw amorous birds

Under this foliage one day.

I was attentive to their sports,

To their sweet jesting.

But the first to fly off

Was the infidel male.

From that moment, I am listening

To the complaints of the female.

PHILINTE:

See: on this flowered shore

That brings together these two streams;

They do it only in the prairie,

Nothing can divide their streams.

Let's join our souls the same way,

By the most pleasant bond;

Helen, in a heart that loves you

Come enmix yours forever.

HELEN:

Shepherd, despite myself, I am afflicting you.

Why, we must stop seeing each other.

If I have some power over you,

This is the proof that I am demanding of it.

PHILINTE:

I'm going to leave,

I'm going to die.

When you hear the sweet zephyr

Make some complaint in these reeds,

Think, think that it's a sigh

Of unhappy Philinte.

On a bough

When the turtledove,

Far from its companion, comes to shiver,

Let Helen think that her absence

Is making me die.

Let the water that's spreading around these flowers,

By its murmur, make you hear how many tears

You are making me shed.

HELEN:

His sorrow is piercing my soul

What power is controlling me!

I'm afraid to listen to his passion

And despite myself I'm staying.

PHILINTE:

If your heart is freeing itself

Can't I know the reason?

HELEN:

Eh! No, no, no,

Don't tell me any more about it.

(Helen leaves.)

PHILINTE:

I've lost my dear Helen.

O sorrow! The ingrate is fleeing me.

Will I be able to forget this inhuman person?

I fear that my soul is following her.

I see my two rivals coming.

What should I do?

Let's hide behind these reeds

So as to hear them.

(Enter Richard and Damon.)

RICHARD:

Go sell your wares elsewhere,

Mr. Amorous Flibbertigibbet,

For there's no food for a bird like you

From a virgin of this village.

DAMON:

I shall be preferred to you.

RICHARD:

That's deluding yourself with a vain hope.

They must reward

Our perseverance.

Fret, swear, here and there,

Helter-skelter,

Hither and thither,

Badabim bada boom, I don't care a hoot about all that.

My sweet shepherdess

Will be my reward.

DAMON:

Yeah? Oh, yeah?

RICHARD:

Although I'm not a gentleman,

In our village they respect me

And no one's more important than me.

I will oppose you.

DAMON:

My friend, I pity you.

But end it, your talk slays me.

Helen loves this clodhopper!

RICHARD:

Keep on boasting. (repeat)

DAMON:

I've reigned in a thousand hearts,

Without taking much trouble,

This one's not much trouble.

RICHARD:

He thinks because he has longed

That all the beauties are impassioned.

Do you pluck hearts

Like milky apples, eh?

I'm sure of having won

That of young Helen.

With us the heart of a mistress

Doesn't surrender so promptly.

Constant sighing is required.

DAMON:

They cut the tenderness short in Paris.

It's the work of a moment.

Constancy weakens taste

And change awakens it.

Like the industrious bee

I know how to take everything from the flower.

RICHARD:

With that fine system

Does he expect to render

His beauty very tender?

All will laugh at a Flibbertigibbet,

Or flee him like a monster.

I see her coming down the hill.

She will explain herself between the two of us.

DAMON:

It's not you Helen will choose.

RICHARD:

Ha! Ha! We're going to see about that.

(Enter Helen.)

HELEN:

I vainly moved away

From this fountain.

By its shores, a tender lover

Shivers in pain.

Love insensibly

Always brings me back,

Always brings me back.

RICHARD:

(catching her) Your servant.

DAMON:

Come, little one.

She's as pretty as a beautiful day.

The sight of her excites in every heart

Desires, distractions of love.

I hope, also, that today

Yours will surrender to my merit.

RICHARD:

—He—he's trapping her,

He's trapping her.

DAMON:

Calm the lively burning

Of the passion that excites me.

Why this blush?

HELEN:

Sir?

DAMON:

I adore you,

Honor bright.

Still modest.

Fie, that's horrible.

RICHARD:

The sight of you afflicts her.

DAMON:

You are lowering your eyes.

RICHARD:

I am furious, I mean really, really furious, I tell you.

Zounds, his fury's going to freeze his heart.

DAMON:

When you make it with me,

You will shine

In a fashionable outfit.

Let's hurry to marry.

Let this kiss

Be the pledge.

HELEN:

(repulsing Damon) Take it easy, no joking.

RICHARD AND HELEN:

That's not done.

That's not suitable.

RICHARD:

Once you're my housekeeper,

I will kick out of our home

All these pipsqueaks that displease you.

DAMON:

He's a brute, a jealous type.

RICHARD:

If I have some quarrel,

That will only put new life in our relationship.

Zounds, they call that

Recoiling to jump better.

The two of us will retire to our farm,

I'll do nothing but make better love.

I won't rent you a carriage.

What's the use of a fuss?

But every day will be a wedding day.

Bestir yourself,

Bestir yourself, my babe,

For my love is steadier

Than that of all the gentlemen of the court.

DAMON:

Must he be so proud,

Especially with a Lord?

Helen's the first

With whom I've experienced coldness,

Mommy, mommy.

Mom, mom, dear mommy,

It's miserable

To keep me in pain.

HELEN:

Do you know our rules?

Do you know our rules?

Naive love reigns in our woods.

Our hearts only listen to his voice,

The sincere lover obtains his rights.

Only he deserves our choice,

Our discussion has no greater burden.

Interest is out of it,

Our feelings only

Emerge from a pure source.

Here we love artlessly

Everything naturally.

DAMON:

Pick me, my pretty,

There's nobody as frank as me.

RICHARD:

You will find in my person

A very natural, good love.

TOGETHER:

Ah! My dear mistress!

DAMON:

So answer to my tenderness.

RICHARD:

So answer to my tenderness;

For she's my sole desire,

'Cause, hold on, that's what gives me the greatest pleasure.

DAMON:

Don't listen to this working stiff.

He'll take umbrage at the first word.

RICHARD:

Don't listen to the prattle

Of this little Flibbertigibbet

Ah! Really, a fine bird!

What would you have in common with him?

Ah! Really, a fine bird

That you would have for a lover!

The Nightingale makes its singing

So long as it enjoys its liberty.

But if it's in a cage, it shuts up

And nothing awakens its gaiety.

That's the image of a little dandy.

First he loves to excess,

He sings before the marriage,

But you never hear him sing afterwards.

DAMON:

When love is tired of the household,

Liberty compensates us.

It's only in the homes of the bourgeoisie

That marriage is slavery.

Now they experience, under its sway,

All the bitterness of widowhood.

RICHARD:

Let's cut off this superfluous discussion

And let Helen decide between us.

HELEN:

I'm in love, I cannot deny it any more.

Forgive a timid heart,

But I'm afraid, by naming a spouse,

Of the wrath of a jealous rival.

DAMON:

A heart is its own master.

RICHARD:

Love alone must rule.

PHILINTE:

(aside, at the back of the stage)

What have I heard?

DAMON AND RICHARD:

(aside) I'm the one she loves.

PHILINTE:

She's going to choose someone else.

DAMON:

My heart, have no care,

I know how to protect you.

RICHARD:

I'll know how to protect it, too.

PHILINTE:

(to Lisette at the back of the stage) Lisette, come listen.

Just gods! Ungrateful Helen,

I am going to expire before her eyes.

(Enter Philinte and Lisette.)

HELEN:

At this time I'm going to make

A sincere confession.

Both of you take an oath

To see my choice without anger.

RICHARD:

Yes, pronounce it boldly.

PHILINTE:

(still not seen)

O heaven!

DAMON:

Name your lover.

HELEN:

(choosing Philinte whom she has noticed)

Here's the one I prefer.

PHILINTE:

I've won.

I can hardly believe it.

HELEN:

Dry your tears,

Our fears are ending,

Our pleasures beginning.

Let's join our hearts.

(to Damon) A heart is its own master.

(to Richard) Love alone must rule.

Both of you, follow your system,

You must guarantee my choice

RICHARD:

Zounds, this beats all.

HELEN:

(to Richard) You love too much.

(to Damon) And you, too little.

I don't want for my husband

Either an inconstant or a jealous type.

DAMON:

On my word, this decision is delightful.

Richard shakes and is desolated.

As for me, I'm doing better.

No goodbyes, adorable shepherdess,

I'll be expecting you at the end of a month or so.

The stupidity of a choosing a shepherd

While scorning an agreeable Lord!

Word of a Chevalier, that is,

Singular taste.

Indeed, indeed, very singular

Indeed, indeed, very singular.

(Damon leaves.)

RICHARD:

Zounds, let's avenge ourselves

For their treacherous passion.

PHILINTE:

I was worried about your tenderness,

I'm not very worried about your wrath.

RICHARD:

Let her watch out for her, Philinte.

Why bother myself so much?

With the sweet juice of my brew

I'm going to console myself.

(Richard leaves.)

LISETTE:

Everything answers to your wish.

You must give yourself up to pleasure.

The troupe of shepherds is coming forward.

Under this cool shade, they are going

To award the prize of confidence

To these most perfect lovers.

(Lisette leaves.)

HELEN:

Will you forgive me, Philinte

For having tried your heart?

Your rivals were making me frightened.

I was scared of their fury.

By an innocent trick

I am crowning your passion.

PHILINTE:

If the passions of all lovers

And their most ardent distractions

Were joined in my soul,

Helen, o my most dear treasure,

They still couldn't pay

For a spark from your flame.

DUO:

Let our charming fetters

Serve as models

To perfect lovers;

Amorous shepherds

Crown the passion

Of two faithful hearts.

PHILINTE:

Love, may your favors

Have delights for us!

HELEN:

Love make eternal

Our sincere passions.

TOGETHER:

Let our charming fetters

Serve as models

To perfect lovers.

Amorous shepherds

Crown the passion

Of two faithful hearts.

DIVERSION

(Shepherds and shepherdesses descend, two by two from the hill. The shepherds present a crown to Helen, and the shepherdesses a crown to Philinte.)

PHILINTE:

On this day, tender bagpipes

Repeat the echo of your accents.

Helen finally is engaged

And shares my ardent transports.

You don't dare complain,

Nor depict my languor to her.

My sighs, after so many troubles,

Helen allows the singing of my pleasures.

A SHEPHERD:

(singing to the same refrain)

The shepherdess who entices me

Is afraid of the language

Of Love.

It's necessary that my bagpipe,

Most discreetly,

Express in its turn

What I make heard

With a tender tune.

The amorous accords,

My dear Themire,

Sighs

And seems sensible to my passion.

A SHEPHERDESS:

The shepherd Silvandre

Doesn't dare tell me of his passion.

He is silent, but his bagpipe

Is the interpreter of his heart.

How dangerous it is to hear it!

I'm afraid of listening to its accents

And I won't know how to protect myself.

Alas! With what powerful charms

The enchanter knows how to surprise me.

He troubles, he enchains my senses.

The shepherd Silvandre

Doesn't dare to tell me of his passion.

He is silent, but his bagpipe

Is the interpreter of his heart.

I am dreaming, I am distracted,

When I hear his tunes.

Without thinking about it, I repeat them in a murmur,

And despite myself, my indiscreet voice

Rises and joins in his tunes.

The shepherd Silvandre

Doesn't dare tell me of his passion.

He is silent, but his bagpipe

Is the interpreter of his heart.

CURTAIN

ABOUT THE EDITOR

Frank J. Morlock has written and translated many plays since retiring from the legal profession in 1992. His translations have also appeared on Project Gutenberg, the Alexandre Dumas Père web page, Literature in the Age of Napoléon, Infinite Artistries.com, and Munsey's (formerly Blackmask). In 2006 he received an award from the North American Jules Verne Society for his translations of Verne's plays. He lives and works in México.

www.ingramcontent.com/pod-product-compliance
Lightning Source LLC
LaVergne TN
LVHW041616070426
835507LV00008B/275